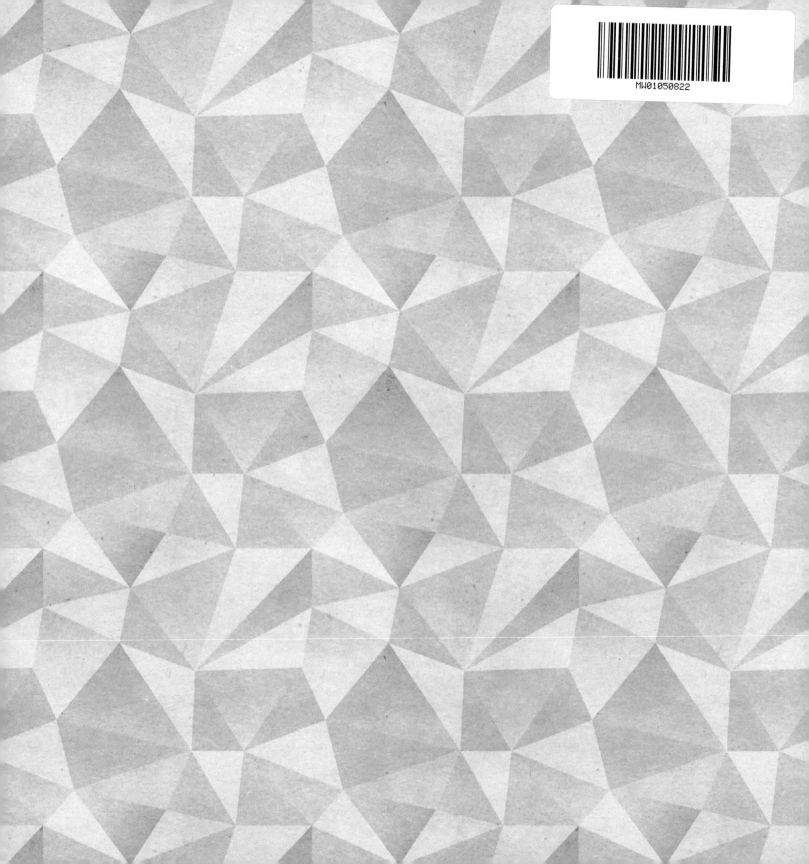

Quarto is the authority on a wide range of topics.
Quarto educates, entertains, and enriches the lives of our readers—
enthusiasts and lovers of hands-on living.
www.quartoknows.com

Written by Tricia Martineau Wagner
Illustrated by Carles Ballesteros

6 Orchard Road, Suite 100
Lake Forest, CA 92630
quartoknows.com
Visit our blogs at quartoknows.com

Printed in China
1 3 5 7 9 10 8 6 4 2

MIX
Paper from
responsible sources
FSC® C104723

50
WACKY
THINGS
ANIMALS DO

Weird & amazing animal facts!

Walter Foster
Jr.

Written by Tricia Martineau Wagner
Illustrated by Carles Ballesteros

TABLE OF CONTENTS

THE ODD SQUAD

Do you swim inside a shark's mouth for your dinner?
Can you clean out your ears with your tongue?

We certainly hope not!

But there are animals that do these and other incredibly wacky things. And you can read all about them right here.

Skunks doing handstands?
Yes.

Herring talking with toots?
Of course!

Tiptoeing horses and fainting goats?
Why not?!

You'll also discover why these bizarre behaviors are actually perfectly normal for each of these animals. They only seem wacky to us! So prepare for a peculiar parade of vomiting vultures, escaping octopuses, kicking kangaroos, freezing frogs, and much, much more.

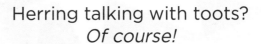

NO. 1
FOOD FOR THOUGHT

Food passes through a giant squid's brain before it makes its way to its stomach. Now that's a brainy idea! The squid has a tiny brain shaped like a doughnut. The *esophagus*, or food tube, runs through the hole. The squid grabs fish with its sharp-hooked tentacles, and its powerful beak tears the fish apart. Then the tiny pieces are fed through the brain.

MORE ABOUT SQUIDS

The colossal squid lives in the deep, cold waters around the southern tip of Africa down to Antarctica. The cold temperatures make the squid digest food slowly so it does not need much food. Colossal squids weigh up to 1,600 pounds (725 kilograms) and can grow up to 46 feet (14 meters) long. That's longer than a school bus!

NO. 2
SLUGGISH SLOTHS

It's a good thing sloths don't have to go to school—
they'd never make it on time! These drowsy tree
dwellers move very, very slowly. When awake,
they only travel an average of 9 feet (3 meters)
per minute. In fact, they are so incredibly slow
that green algae, which are plant-like organisms,
actually grow on their fur.

MORE ABOUT SLOTHS

Sloths live in the jungles of Central and South America
and spend most of their time hanging from tree
branches. The green algae in their fur help hide them
from predators. The algae, along with the insects that live
in their fur, also provide tasty snacks.

NO. 3
LAZY BIRDS

If you were not related to a cuckoo bird, you would end up doing all of its chores! Cuckoo birds are so lazy that they don't even raise their own children. Instead, female cuckoos lay their eggs in other birds' nests. And even though the baby cuckoo hatchlings look nothing like the other baby birds in the nest, their new parents still care for them.

MORE ABOUT CUCKOO BIRDS
Cuckoo birds live in Europe, Africa, Asia, and Australia. A newly hatched cuckoo bird will often try to push the unhatched eggs out of the nest so it can eat more of the food. Yet each year, different birds accept cuckoo eggs in their nests.

NO. 4
SCAREDY GOATS

If someone comes up behind you and yells "boo!," your muscles will tense up for a moment. If you scare a Tennessee Fainting Goat, the same thing happens... except it's much worse. As the goat begins to run away, its muscles completely freeze up, and it falls on its back or side. After about ten seconds, the goat can get up and move around again.

MORE ABOUT TENNESSEE FAINTING GOATS

These goats aren't actually fainting—they just lose their ability to run as their muscles freeze up. This condition isn't too much of a problem on a farm, but they wouldn't last long in the wild!

NO. 5
AMAZING ARCHITECTS

Male Australian bowerbirds build dazzling nests, called *bowers*, in the forest to attract female mates. These twig structures can be up to 6 feet wide (1.8 meters). The male bowerbird spends months building and decorating the bower with colorful berries, stones, feathers, and pieces of plastic or coins. He even steals from or destroys other bowers so his looks better.

MORE ABOUT BOWERBIRDS

The male bowerbird works hard for love. If a female likes his bower, he performs a funny dance to win the female's heart. After mating, the female leaves the bower, builds her own nest in the trees, and raises her young alone.

NO. 6
STINKY DANCERS

This silly sight should give you a fright! When a spotted skunk feels trouble is near, it will stand on its front paws, dance, and wave its tail. This isn't so you will die laughing—the handstand makes the skunk looks bigger and more dangerous. If a predator isn't smart enough to heed this warning, the skunk will squirt a stinky spray that can cause temporary blindness and nausea.

MORE ABOUT SPOTTED SKUNKS

The spotted skunk lives in the southern half of North America. The skunk's spray sac gives off five squirts, and it takes about a week to produce new spray. That's why they dance first, and spray only if they are in real danger.

NO. 7
TIPPY TOES

Can you win a race running on your tippy toes? Horses do! Each foot has a single large toe and two smaller toes, and the smaller toes don't touch the ground when the horse runs. They are connected to the big toe and give it support to prevent the horse from twisting its foot while running.

MORE ABOUT HORSES

Horse's toes are covered by a thick, tough toenail called a *hoof*. The hoof makes contact with the ground. Horses need to have their hooves trimmed often. Special instruments called hoof nippers and rasps are used to clip and file the hooves.

NO. 8
UPSIDE-DOWN DINNER

It's a good thing you are not a flamingo, otherwise you would have to eat with your head upside-down. Flamingos use their large lower beak to strain water and mud from the food they find. This *filter feeding* helps them gulp up a mouthful of algae, shrimp, fish, and insects.

MORE ABOUT FLAMINGOS

Flamingos can live in both warm and colder climates. They just need plenty of water and mud. These birds stomp their webbed feet to stir up food. They also sweep their heads below the water to loosen food from the mud.

NO. 9
CRAB CAMOUFLAGE

The fearsome-looking Japanese spider crab looks like something out of a scary movie. But don't worry. It's mostly a gentle creature that would rather hide than fight. That's why it attaches sea creatures, such as sponges, anemones, and kelp to its body. As the crab looks for food on the ocean floor, the creature camouflage hides it from predators above.

MORE ABOUT JAPANESE SPIDER CRABS

The male Japanese spider crab's leg span is 12 feet (4 meters) from claw to claw—the longest of all *arthropods,* or animals that have hard outside coverings. But its body is only 16 inches (40 centimeters) across. These crabs are found in the deep waters around Japan, and may live to be 100 years old. Its Japanese name, *Taka-ashi-gani*, means "tall legs crab."

NO. 10
COW MAGNETS

Lost? Well, you don't need a compass to find north and south. Just locate some hungry cows! Earth's magnetic poles make a compass needle point north and south. But the poles seem to make cows' heads turn as well. When eating or resting, cows line up in a north-south direction according to Earth's magnetic field. And they swivel their heads north or south when grazing.

MORE ABOUT COWS
Scientists used satellite images to look down on cattle from high above Earth. They studied 8,000 head of cattle around the world. Scientists also discovered that deer do the same thing when grazing or resting.

NO. 11
POTTY MOUTH

If you see a Chinese soft-shelled turtle spitting, it's probably not water. This turtle pees through its mouth. Eww! Peeing the normal way takes a lot of water, and since these turtles live in salty water that they can't drink, they need to conserve water any way they can. To clean their mouth, all they have to do is rinse with the salty water and spit.

MORE ABOUT CHINESE SOFT-SHELL TURTLES

This turtle is the only known animal that pees this way. It lives in and around China, and has also been introduced to other countries, including the United States. It is found in rivers, lakes, ponds, creeks, canals, and marshes.

NO. 12
A ROCKY MARRIAGE

Women often get a diamond ring when getting engaged to be married. But not penguins. The male Adélie penguin searches for the perfect stone or pebble for his mate. Once he finds it, he waddles over and drops the stone offering at the female penguin's feet. She must then decide if she likes the gift. If so, she will use the treasured pebble when building her nest.

MORE ABOUT ADÉLIE PENGUINS

Adélie penguins live in Antarctica near the South Pole. They have a thick layer of fat under their feathered coats to keep them warm. Penguins waddle on their webbed feet, but sliding on their bellies across the ice is a much faster—and more fun—way to travel.

NO. 13
LYING LYREBIRDS

You're in the middle of the Australian woods, miles from civilization, when you suddenly hear a baby crying his head off. Huh?! Don't be fooled! It may just be a lyrebird. This bird is an expert at reproducing sounds it has heard before. It can perfectly mimic a koala, a car alarm, a chainsaw, or even a crying baby. It's hard to tell the difference between the imitations and the real sounds.

MORE ABOUT LYREBIRDS

The lyrebird is one of the best-known birds in Australia. The males have large, beautiful tails that they fan out during mating season. They can live up to 30 years, and have existed for at least 15 million years.

NO. 14
FREEZING FROGS

Can you imagine freezing during the cold winter and thawing out in the warm spring? That is exactly what the North American wood frog does! It survives winter with more than half of its body's water turned to ice. The frog buries itself underground and goes into a deep hibernation for two to three months. During winter, the wood frog's breathing and heartbeat stop, but it doesn't die.

MORE ABOUT NORTH AMERICAN WOOD FROGS
The North American wood frog is one of the few frogs that can survive in Alaska and above the Arctic Circle. When frozen, the frog's body temperature ranges from 21 to 30 degrees Fahrenheit (-6 to -1 degrees Celsius). Come spring, the frog warms up and its heart starts beating again.

NO. 15
BIG BABY BINKY

An elephant uses its trunk for smelling, breathing, squirting water, feeding itself, picking up objects, and exploring its environment. Elephants even use their trunks to hug each other. But baby elephants, called *calves*, suck their trunks when they are scared, cranky, or tired. They may weigh 200 pounds (100 kilograms), but they need comfort just like human babies do.

MORE ABOUT ELEPHANTS

There are two types of elephants: the Asian elephant and the African elephant. African elephants are the largest land mammals. An elephant's trunk has 100,000 muscles, can grow up to 6 feet long (2 meters), and can weigh up to 308 pounds (140 kilograms).

NO. 16
TURTLE TEARS

Butterflies spend a lot of time hovering around yellow spotted river turtles. What do they want? Turtle tears! The fluid that wells up in these turtles' eyes is salty. Since the butterflies need that salt to live, they excitedly swarm around the turtles' heads to sip the tears.

MORE ABOUT YELLOW SPOTTED RIVER TURTLES

Yellow spotted river turtles live in the Amazon rain forest. These meat-eating turtles get all the salt they need from their diet. The butterflies, however, don't get enough salt from their diet of plant nectar. That's why they go after the turtle tears. Scientists don't think this process hurts the turtles, but they aren't 100-percent sure yet.

NO. 17
WET WIGGLES

Giraffes have a wacky way of cleaning their ears—they use their very long tongues! Giraffes use their tongues to reach acacia leaves high up in the trees, but when they have an itch in their ear, their tongues reach in and give it a wet wiggle. An adult male giraffe's tongue can be up to 21 inches (53 centimeters) long.

MORE ABOUT GIRAFFES

Giraffes live in savanna areas in Africa and are the tallest mammals in the world. Many people once thought giraffes were a cross between a leopard and a camel. However, its only known relative is the *okapi*, which looks a little like a zebra.

NO. 18
PLAYING DEAD

Opossums aren't good at fighting back, but they can fool their enemies by playing dead. Danger makes an opossum go into a shock-like state where its body freezes up. Its stiff body will lay sideways with legs out and mouth open. The opossum even releases a green, stinky fluid that smells like a dead, rotting animal. Since many predators are used to chasing their prey, they leave the "dead" opossum alone.

MORE ABOUT OPOSSUMS

A "dead" opossum will stay unconscious for up to four hours. Before playing dead, an opossum hisses and growls at predators. It produces extra saliva in its mouth, then blows the drool out of its nose, hoping the bubbles make it look sick and not like a good snack.

NO. 19
ALL PUFFED UP

Pufferfish should be an easy meal for predators. (They are slow, clumsy swimmers.) But they have a clever way of scaring away enemies. Pufferfish suck in water and blow themselves up to several times their original size. Suddenly, what looked like a good meal is now a giant, scary water balloon with eyes and fins. They can stay inflated for 15 minutes, then they need to rest for five hours afterward.

MORE ABOUT PUFFERFISH

Pufferfish live mostly in tropical and subtropical waters. They are extremely poisonous. But that doesn't stop trained chefs from removing the poisonous parts and preparing *fugu*, a tasty (but risky) Japanese dish.

NO. 20
VULTURE VOMIT

Look out if vultures feel threatened! Vultures feed on *carcasses*, or dead animal bodies. This helps clean up roadkill on streets and highways. But any predator coming after a vulture while it's eating is in for a surprise. The vulture will vomit in the direction of the enemy. Emptying its stomach lightens it, so it can quickly fly away.

MORE ABOUT VULTURES

Vultures do not have strong feet or beaks, so they can't carry food back to their nests for their hungry offspring. Therefore, vultures eat food and regurgitate, or throw up, the food to feed their young.

NO. 21
FISH FLOSSERS

Would you swim inside a shark's mouth? Most fish swim far away when sharks come around, but pilot fish don't! Pilot fish actually swim inside a shark's mouth, and act as a shark toothbrush. They never have to worry about becoming the shark's next meal because the shark leaves the fish alone in return for the teeth cleaning.

MORE ABOUT PILOT FISH

Pilot fish nibble away at food particles stuck between sharks' teeth. They also eat harmful parasites that would make the sharks sick. When not darting in and out of a shark's mouth, pilot fish swim underneath the shark, making it difficult for other predators to catch them.

NO. 22
ARMOR BALL

The Chinese pangolin can turn into an armored bowling ball. If it senses danger, it will roll into a spiked ball to protect itself. This four-legged creature has a pointed head, a long, thick tail, and brown scales. Never mistake a Chinese pangolin for a ball and try to pick it up. Its pointy scales are razor sharp!

MORE ABOUT PANGOLINS

The Chinese pangolin is found in southeast China. The word *pangolin* comes from a Malayan word meaning roller. Even though the Chinese pangolin is not closely related to the anteater, it only eats ants and termites.

NO. 23
SIMPLY SHOCKING

Don't mess with an electric eel or you're in for a jolt! They can deliver a series of powerful electric shock waves. The shock gives a short, numbing pain that stops muscle movement. Their 500-volt shock can kill smaller animals and hurt larger ones. The eel's "stun gun" can even numb an alligator with its powerful punch.

MORE ABOUT ELECTRIC EELS

An electric eel can grow up to 6 feet (2 meters) long. It is not actually an eel, but rather a fish called a *knifefish*. It has three pairs of organs in its stomach that produce electricity.

NO. 24
BRAVE TAILS

Most animals steer clear of rattlesnakes. But not the California ground squirrel. These brave squirrels even tease and taunt rattlesnakes by wagging their tails back and forth. Sometimes they will even lunge at an uncoiled snake. Other times they kick sand in the snake's eyes.

MORE ABOUT CALIFORNIA GROUND SQUIRRELS

The squirrel's zigzag run helps it avoid a snake's attack. If bitten, adult squirrels have developed some resistance to snake venom. However, rattlesnakes like to surprise their prey. So once the California ground squirrel shakes its tail to tell the snake it's aware of its presence, the snake becomes less interested in attacking.

NO. 25
MOUTH GUARD

It may look like a mother tilapia is eating all of her babies, but don't be fooled. When the mother tilapia senses danger, she will suck her young into her mouth, where the tiny fish swim inside and hide. When it's safe, the mother will release them back into the water.

MORE ABOUT TILAPIA

Tilapia are native to the warm waters around Africa. The mother fish inhales her young and then spits them out repeatedly. This gives the baby fish a better chance of growing to adulthood. The mother will also keep her eggs in her mouth before they hatch.

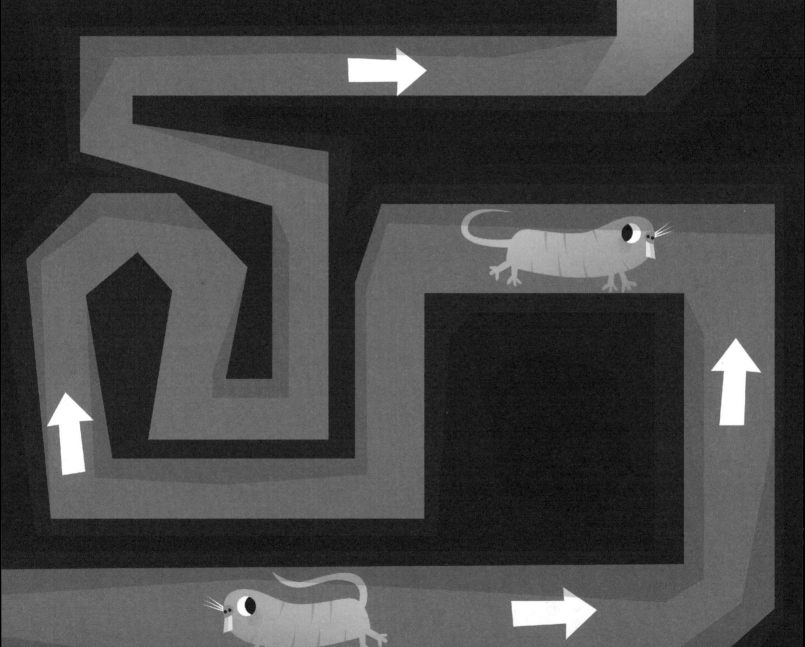

FINISH

NO. 26
RODENTS IN REVERSE

Naked mole rats aren't naked, although they have very little hair. They aren't moles or rats either. They are, however, funny-looking rodents that live almost their entire lives underground, running back and forth through mazes of tight underground tunnels. And they are the only mammals that can run just as quickly backward or forward—without having to turn around!

MORE ABOUT NAKED MOLE RATS

These tiny critters live in the deserts of East Africa. They have pink, wrinkly skin and thin ratlike tails. Their tube-shaped bodies are almost hairless. Naked mole rats are closely related to porcupines, chinchillas, and guinea pigs.

NO. 27
BLOODSHOT EYES

Don't get too close to a horned lizard. They have a scary way of protecting themselves. If threatened, horned lizards can shoot a stream of blood out from their eyes. The blood can squirt up to five feet (1.5 meters), causing confusion in their enemies. The blood has no poison, but it tastes horrible.

MORE ABOUT HORNED LIZARDS

Horned lizards live in the Southwestern United States. They are sometimes called horny toads because their flattened, round bodies make them look like toads. If in danger, a horned lizard can also suck in air to expand like a balloon. This makes the lizard look bigger and scarier than it really is.

NO. 28
NOSE BALLOONS

For male hooded seals, balloons aren't for birthday parties or celebrations. They are used to attract a female mate and scare off the competition. If more than one male is interested in a female, they will face off not by fighting, but by blowing a huge red or pink balloon out of their left nostril—the bigger, the better! Once there is only one male seal left, he will try to win the female over with his big nose balloon.

MORE ABOUT HOODED SEALS

Hooded seals live in the North Atlantic and Arctic Oceans. Males can grow up to six feet (1.8 meters) long and 900 pounds (408 kilograms). They are silver with dark, irregular marks. The nose balloon is not a giant booger. It is actually a piece of skin, called a *membrane*, filled with air.

NO. 29
ICE KINGS

Arctic walruses are known to fight for a spot on their favorite ice sheets—even if there's room for everyone. A pack of fifty or more walruses will wrestle and push each other until only the strongest walrus remains on the floating island. The winner basks in the sun all by itself.

MORE ABOUT ARCTIC WALRUSES

Walruses live in the cold Arctic by the North Pole. Males weighing up to 2,700 pounds (1,225 kilograms) will also attack each other using their up to three-foot-long (.9 meter) tusks. Their thick skin comes in handy during fights, but doesn't always protect them from getting hurt. They also use their tusks to cut through ice and to get their giant bodies out of the water.

NO. 30
BE DAZZLED

Imagine you're a little fish in the ocean and a much bigger fish is coming at you fast. You think you can get away, but suddenly this dull gray-blue fish changes colors in a flash. Now it's light blue with bright yellow stripes. Before you can even understand what's happening, you're dinner. The sailfish isn't simply one of the fastest fish in the ocean—it also changes colors instantly to confuse its prey. Good luck, fish!

MORE ABOUT SAILFISH

Sailfish live in warmer waters in oceans all around the world. They are also known as *billfish* because they have long, sword-like bills that they use when hunting. Their *dorsal fins*, or the fins on their backs, look like a sail, which is where they get their name. They change colors when excited, such as when they are hunting.

NO. 31
GRIZZLY GUT

Squirrels bury nuts in the ground so they have food for the winter. Grizzly bears store food as well—in their stomachs. They eat up to 90 pounds (40 kilograms) of food a day during the warmer months, and they live off the extra fat while hibernating in the winter. That's a whole lot of food to store!

MORE ABOUT GRIZZLIES

Known as the North American brown bear, grizzlies are mostly found in Canada and Alaska. They eat nuts, fruit, fungi, insects, fish, rodents, sheep, and elk. Female grizzlies weigh up to 800 pounds (363 kilograms), and males weigh up to 1,700 pounds (771 kilograms).

NO. 32
UNFLAPPABLE

Wings that don't have to flap for hundreds of miles? No wonder the albatross can fly thousands of miles without stopping. It can even nap while flying! It dozes off while gliding at 25 miles (40 kilometers) per hour. Hopefully it watches out for mountains!

MORE ABOUT ALBATROSSES

Albatrosses are among the largest of flying birds with wingspans reaching up to 12 feet (3.7 meters). The special way they angle their wings to take advantage of wind patterns means they can fly more than 600 miles (1,000 kilometers) without flapping their wings.

NO. 33
TURNING HEADS

What if teachers could turn their heads like owls? They would see everything their classes were up to while writing on the board. Owls can almost rotate their heads in a complete circle. This is helpful because, unlike lots of other animals, they cannot move their eyes. That means in order to see something next to it, an owl has to turn its head.

MORE ABOUT OWLS

Owls can be found in most parts of the world, and in many different habitats. There are more than 200 different species of owls. They are great hunters with good eyesight, sharp claws, and wings that help them fly silently.

NO. 34
GAS PASSERS

Did you hear that? The herring communicates by passing gas. They blow bubbles out of their rear ends. However, unlike our gas, theirs doesn't drive friends away—it brings them closer. The herring hear the toots and use the sound to draw closer together at night. Scientists have called this method of communication *Fast Repetitive Tick*... FART for short.

MORE ABOUT HERRING

Herring often live together in large groups, called *schools*, and can be found in the northern Atlantic and Pacific Oceans. They are a source of food for bigger fish, seabirds, dolphins, whales, seals, and humans.

NO. 35
NINE LIVES

Cats have been said to have nine lives. Maybe it's because they can survive falls from great heights and rarely seem to get hurt. Cats have good balance, and they are usually awesome climbers. But sometimes they tumble. Cats fall from trees, off balconies, and out of windows. But somehow our furry friends always land on their feet.

MORE ABOUT CATS

Cats have what's called a *righting reflex*. This allows them to twist in midair when falling. Cats also spread out their legs to create a parachute shape with their bodies. This slows them down and gives them time to twist and land on their feet.

NO. 36
UNLIKELY FRIENDS

Would you let a bunch of birds hang out all day on your back? Rhinoceroses are perfectly happy giving oxpeckers a free ride. Oxpecker birds eat parasites off the rhinoceros. This keeps the rhinoceros healthy, and the oxpecker birds don't have to look hard for food—it's right on top of the rhino's skin!

MORE ABOUT RHINOCEROSES

Rhinoceroses live in Africa and Asia. The oxpecker and rhinoceros enjoy a *symbiotic relationship*, which means they live together, and each animal gets something good from the other. Oxpeckers will also hiss and scream if they see a predator coming. This gives rhinos time to react.

NO. 37
REPTILIAN WORKOUT

The western sagebrush lizard keeps in good shape with push-ups! Male lizards bask in the hot sun soaking up the rays. But as soon as a female lizard comes strolling by, the male goes into action. It raises its body up off the ground over and over again in push-up style. This displays his colorful underbelly, which attracts the female.

MORE ABOUT THE WESTERN SAGEBRUSH LIZARD

The underbelly and throat of the western sagebrush lizard have a striking, shiny blue patch separated by a white stripe. The male lizard waits until a female comes within a 4-inch (10-centimeter) distance before "exercising" so the female will notice his bright colors better.

NO. 38
BACKWARD BILBY

You probably know about kangaroo pouches. Just like kangaroos, Australian bilbies also carry their babies in a pouch until they are ready to survive on their own. But bilbies' pouches are backward! The backward pouch keeps any dirt from getting inside while the bilby moms dig or burrow underground.

MORE ABOUT BILBIES

Female Australian bilbies carry two babies in their pouches for up to 80 days. The bilby is a protected species in Australia. Chocolate long-eared bilbies are sold at Easter time to raise money to help protect bilbies.

NO. 39
TONGUE TWISTER

You'd be lucky if you had a tongue like a chameleon. Then you could sneak a lick from someone else's ice cream cone. A chameleon's tongue is twice the length of its body. So stay more than twice as far away, because chameleons can capture their prey with stunning speed. Their tongues can reach their dinner in .07 seconds, which is faster than you can blink.

MORE ABOUT CHAMELEONS

The tip of a chameleon's tongue is a bulb-like ball of muscle that acts like a suction cup. When a chameleon's tongue hits its prey, the tip grabs on and does not let go. Zip! Dinner is ready.

NO. 40
ROCK CHOMPERS

How can you chew food without any teeth? Platypuses don't have teeth inside their bills, but they have a clever way of chewing. To break down food into smaller bits, these bottom-feeders scoop up gravel from the riverbed and keep the pebbles in their cheek pouches. The small stones help grind up insects, worms, and shellfish before the platypus swallows.

MORE ABOUT PLATYPUSES

Platypuses live in the river waters of eastern Australia. They have a large flat bill and a paddle-like tail. The platypus comes to the surface of the water to munch away at its meal with its pretend teeth.

NO. 41
POOP PROTECTORS

Adult Komodo dragons will eat their young if they are hungry, so young Komodo dragons live in the trees for nine months. They come down to the ground when they are big enough to fight off older dragons. The young Komodo dragons also have a good trick if attacked while on the ground—they roll in dragon *dung*, or poop. Adults don't like the stink and stay away.

MORE ABOUT KOMODO DRAGONS

Wild Komodo dragons live only on Indonesia's Lesser Sunda Islands. They are the largest and heaviest lizards on Earth. These giant reptiles can weigh between 150 and 300 pounds (68 and 140 kilograms) and have a clumsy back-and-forth waddle.

NO. 42
OTTERLY FUN

River otters enjoy swimming underwater. But what happens when temperatures drop and rivers freeze? Otters just slide on the ice! River otters are playful animals. They straighten out their bodies and slide great distances on their bellies. River otters enjoy water whether it's wet or frozen.

MORE ABOUT OTTERS

River otters live in rivers and lakes in the United States. Since they do not hibernate during the winter, river otters swim underneath frozen waters to find food. They come to the surface where the ice breaks to breathe.

NO. 43
YOGA BEAR

Giant panda bears do handstands to reach the highest spot on a tree. The higher, the better. Why? So they can pee to leave their scent. This marks their territory. Male pandas choose a wide tree as a target. Rough tree bark best captures the panda's scent. Female pandas look for the highest marking because it will belong to the strongest male panda bear.

MORE ABOUT GIANT PANDAS

Giant panda bears are found in China. About 1,600 pandas are left in the wild today. Giant panda bears have six digits on their paws. The extra digit helps them tear apart the bamboo shoots they eat.

NO. 44
PUPPY LOVE

Are prairie dogs in love? They sure like to kiss! Prairie dogs greet each other by touching their lips together. The kiss can last up to ten seconds. Prairie dogs also hold each other's faces in their paws and hug. In fact, the more prairie dogs are watched, the more they kiss and cuddle. And the bigger the audience, the longer the kiss.

MORE ABOUT PRAIRIE DOGS

Prairie dogs live in grasslands in western United States and Mexico. These burrowing rodents build underground tunnel towns and stand guard on aboveground mounds. They have their own language of barks, yips, and chirps that gives details about nearby predators.

NO. 45
RED LIGHT, GREEN LIGHT

Opening hard-shelled nuts is tough for crows, but they don't give up. These smart city birds drop hard nuts and clamshells onto crosswalks on busy streets, then they wait by the roadside for passing cars and trucks to run over them. Once they hear the loud crack and see the cars stop for the red light, crows swoop in and claim their prize.

MORE ABOUT CROWS

Crows can solve problems (such as how to open up nuts) and remember human faces. If a crow encounters mean humans, it teaches other crows to remember them.

NO. 46
ESCAPE ARTIST

Octopuses are great escape artists! They are intelligent animals that can escape from even the smallest opening in a tank's lid at an aquarium. To escape, an octopus will squeeze its squishy, bag-like body, including all eight arms, through the opening. Then it will slither down to the floor and try to make its way back to the ocean.

MORE ABOUT OCTOPUSES

Octopuses have no bones in their bodies. The beak is the only hard part. So its beak must be able to fit through an opening. Then the octopus can squish the rest of its soft body in or out of just about any space.

NO. 47
DUST BUSTER

If you're ever caught in a desert sandstorm, you better have your goggles with you. Otherwise you'll be blinded by blowing sand. Camels, on the other hand, are always prepared. Camels have thick eyebrows and really long eyelashes. They can clamp their long eyelashes together to create a shield over their eyes to keep out all the dust!

MORE ABOUT CAMELS

Camels also have three eyelids. The third eyelid can be closed during a sandstorm as extra protection. Camel's humps are made out of body fat that can be turned to water or energy.

NO. 48
KANGAROO KICKS

Don't ever get in a boxing ring with a kangaroo. They are expert fighters, and you wouldn't stand a chance! Young male kangaroos, known as *jacks*, spend hours jumping and fighting each other. They duke it out with punching, stand-up wrestling, and sometimes hard kicks. Kangaroos often fight over mates and territory.

MORE ABOUT KANGAROOS

Kangaroos are native to Australia's grasslands. But sometimes they'll visit parks and golf courses too. Kangaroos jump, hop, or bounce because their hind legs move together. However, when swimming, their legs can move independently.

NO. 49
SPIT IT OUT

Llamas hum to communicate. If you hear a long, high-pitched hum, back away! The llama isn't humming because it's in a good mood—it's upset. And unhappy llamas spit. They will spit at each other, and they'll even spit at humans too. Their spit smells horrible—you definitely don't want to be hit with it!

MORE ABOUT LLAMAS

A llama's spit is foul smelling because they are *ruminant* animals, which means they have a four-compartment stomach to digest their food. The food *ferments*, or goes through a chemical change, then the llama vomits and chews the food again.

NO. 50
NAP TIME

Does a good nap make you feel better? Sperm whales think so. They take short power naps to recharge their energy. Pods of sperm whales float like large exclamation points in the water. These snoozing mammals rest for up to twelve minutes. Scientists believe they may even dream while napping.

MORE ABOUT SPERM WHALES

The sperm whale is the largest of the toothed whales. Males can grow to be from 50 to 60 feet (15 to 18 meters) long. They also have the largest brain of any animal on Earth. It is more than five times heavier than a human brain.

Also in this series

50 Wacky Inventions Throughout History describes 50 inventions that seem too crazy to be true—but are! Whether useful, entertaining, or just plain silly, these mind-boggling inventions and gadgets will surprise and delight fun-fact lovers of all ages!